Down The Mountain

A Book About The Ever-Changing Soil

Down The Mountain

A Book About The Ever-Changing Soil

By Margaret Farrington Bartlett

With Illustrations By Rhys Caparn

Young Scott Books

New York

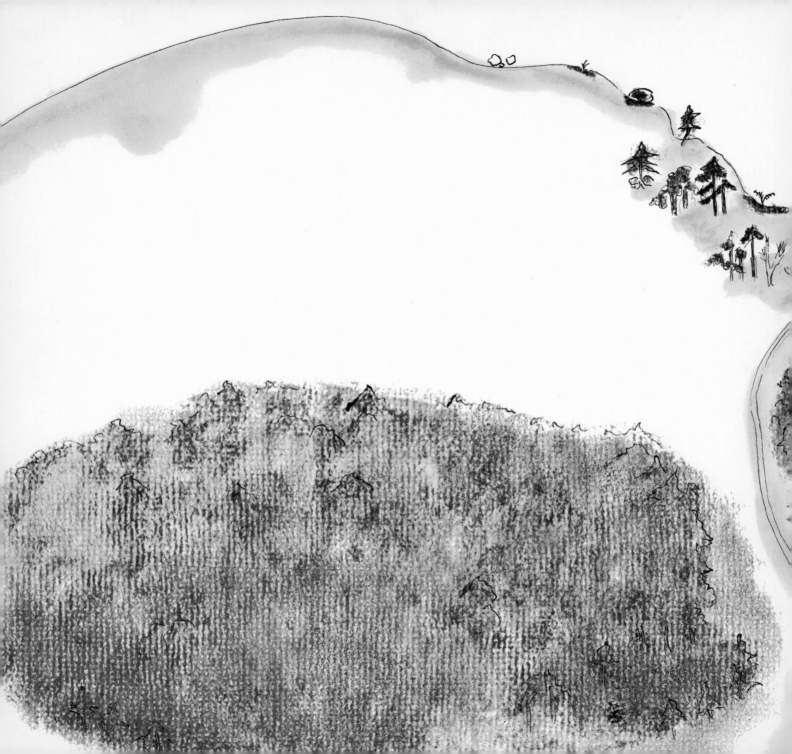

Table of Contents

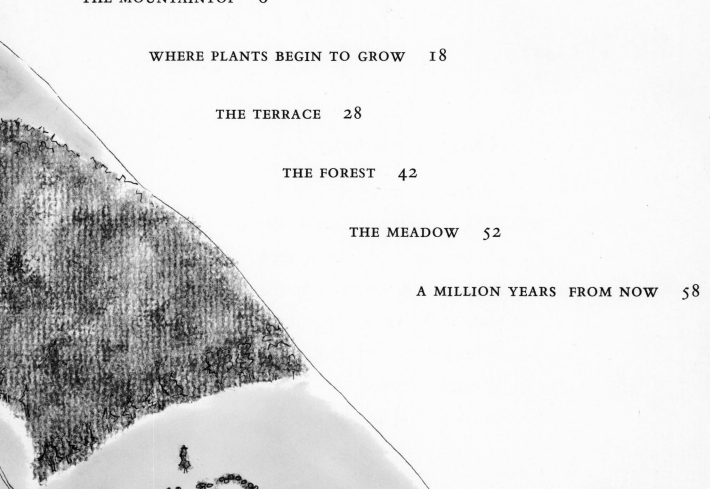

The Mountaintop

Soil covers most of the earth.
In the country, you can see soil
almost everywhere you look.
And there is soil even under the streets
and sidewalks of a big city.
Where does all the soil come from?
We are going to find out
by exploring an old, old mountain.

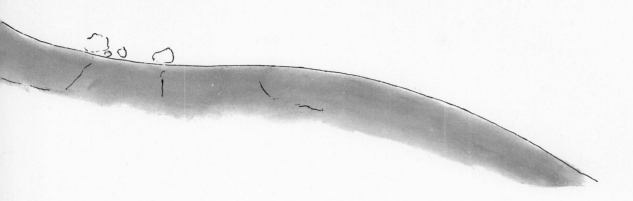

Thick dark forests grow on the mountain,
streams run down its sides.
Every spring, violets and jack-in-the-pulpit
grow in the soil beside the streams.
There are stones and old logs covered with moss.
The mountainside is rich
with blackberries and chokecherries.
But forests and mosses, flowers and berries
did not always grow there.

Millions and millions of years ago,
when the mountain was new,
it was very high—much higher than it is today—
with sharp rocky peaks jutting into the sky.

Nothing grew on the mountainsides then,
because there was no soil for plants to grow in.
The mountain was made of rock alone.
What has made the mountain change
into what it is now?
What has happened to its sharp and jagged peaks?
Where did the soil come from?
You will find the answers to these questions
as we explore the old, old mountain.

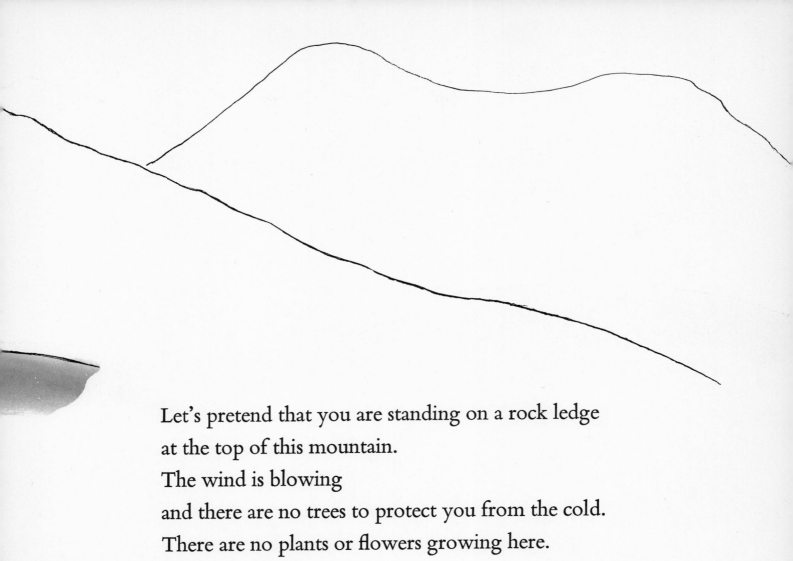

Let's pretend that you are standing on a rock ledge
at the top of this mountain.
The wind is blowing
and there are no trees to protect you from the cold.
There are no plants or flowers growing here.
Where is the soil?

Look down at the rock on which you are standing
and you will see a crack.
Bend down, put your fingers in this crack,
and you will feel a tiny bit of sand.
Are you surprised to find sand
on a rocky mountaintop?

Rain and hail pound against the bare rock in summer.
The sun makes the rock hot and dry.
It is covered by snow and sleet in winter.
The rock is exposed to all kinds of weather.
It is exposed to the rains of spring,
to many, many cold winters and warm summers.
All this time, the forces of the weather
are slowly breaking down the rock.
The rock is being weathered.
The surface of the rock becomes rotted and worn.
Cracks appear in the rock.
Edges of the cracks become weathered and break off.
Little by little the rock breaks down into pieces.
Some pieces are so small that you can hardly see them.
You felt some of those pieces
when you put your fingers in that crack.

Pick up a piece of weathered rock
and look at it carefully.
You can see some of the materials
that the rock is made of.
They are called minerals.
The small bits that look like glass
are a mineral called quartz.
Quartz is very hard—
you cannot break these pieces with your fingers.
Some of the edges
are sharp enough to cut your hand.
In time, after more weathering,
these small pieces of quartz will become sand.
There is sand in soil.
The very small, smooth blocks in your rock
are feldspar, another mineral.

QUARTZ

FELDSPAR

You may see color in the feldspar—
pink, yellow, brown, gray, or milky white.
The small blocks break easily.
When feldspar weathers, it changes to clay.
There is clay in some soil, too.
You might also find, in your piece of rock,
flakes and lumps of another mineral called mica.
The small lumps of mica
are like leaves of a book pressed together.

MICA

When you split the leaves of mica apart,
they break into small flakes.
Many other minerals—such as iron, copper, tin,
and silver—are also found in rock.
But quartz, feldspar, and mica
are the three most important soil-making minerals
that come from the crumbling rock.

On top of the mountain,
you have discovered where sand comes from.
Can you guess how much rock it would take
to make a pailful of sand,
and how long it would take?
It took millions of years of weathering and crumbling
for the new high peak of this mountain to wear down
to the old worn ledge where you are finding the sand.

Do you suppose that all rock on all mountains
is changing to soil?
Yes, it is—little by little.
Every day, every minute, a little soil
is being made from rock.
And wherever you find rock—
on mountains, beside brooks, in fields,
and even beside the road to your house—
the rock is changing to soil.

Where Plants
Begin to Grow

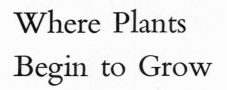

Now, let's move down the steep rock slope
until you see a small plant growing
from a crack in the rock.
Can you guess how the plant got there?

A seed—carried by the wind, dropped by a bird,
or brought on the coat of an animal— fell into the crack.
There was enough mineral food in the crack
(from the quartz, feldspar, and mica)
to nourish the plant.
As the plant grows, its roots dig into the rock,
making tiny tunnels.
As the plant grows bigger,
more tunnels and deeper cracks
are made in the rock.
Water and air seep into the cracks and tunnels.
Now there is more breaking and crumbling of rock.
There is more room for new seeds to survive
and join the soil-making cycle.

There, beside you, is a big loose piece of rock
that probably broke off
from the very top of the mountain.
It is a boulder.
Loose weathered rock does not stay long
on the mountaintop.
The boulder and the rock upon which it now rests
are almost covered with a tiny plant called lichen.
You can easily scrape some lichen
off the rock with your finger.
These tiny plants do not need to take root
in a crack filled with soil.
Their seeds, carried to the rock by the wind,
grow on the surface of rock.
Wherever lichen roots spread,
the rock underneath crumbles and rots.

Here, near the top of the mountain,
there are so few plants to hold the soil
that loose stuff from the weathering boulders,
stones, and gravel are washed down the mountain slope
to even lower places.
This soil material collects in rock hollows.
You can tell where the hollows are
by looking for patches of plant life.

In a hollow, not far from the top of the mountain,
a small scrub pine tree is growing.
Dig around the roots and you will find sand,
small stones, and dusty lumps of clay,
all washed or blown down from the mountaintop.
But there are things around the pine roots
which have not come from the mountain rock.

Look carefully and you will find bits of
crumbled pine bark, partly rotted pine needles,
soft brown cones, all fallen from the tree
and weathered by wind and rain.
These things rot and get mixed together with sand.
This sandy soil is now filled
with mineral from the rock
and soft rotted materials from the pine tree.
When water goes into the soil, it dissolves minerals
and the soft rotted cones and pine needles.
The roots of the pine tree
take nourishment from this sandy soil.
Each year, as cones and needles fall from the pine tree,
they add to the soil—making more food for plants
as they rot and mix with the sand.
Little by little the soil gets richer.

As you go on down the mountain,
the layer of soil grows thicker
because the slope of the mountain is not so steep
and the soil does not wash away so quickly.
It is easier for seeds to grow here.
And where there are more plants,
there are more plant roots to keep the soil
from being washed down the mountain.
Here is another boulder, partly buried in the soil.
The trunk of a pine tree is splitting this boulder.
A seed must have grown in a crack in the rock—
just as one grew in the crack on the mountaintop.
If your fingers could follow the roots,
you would find that they are making cracks and tunnels
through the rock that is under the soil.

Even rock under the soil is changing and breaking down.
And the roots of trees growing down through the soil
help crumble the mountain rock that is under the soil.

A cool wind is blowing now.
You find shelter under a few oak and white pine trees
growing in a hollow place near by.
They grow straight and tall in the sandy soil here,
where they too are sheltered from the wind.
There is an acorn sprouting on the ground
under some old leaves.
The acorn will slowly grow into a new oak tree
as it takes nourishment from the soil.
Blueberry bushes have taken root
in the shelter of some stones.
Every fall their leaves and fruit will add to the soil.

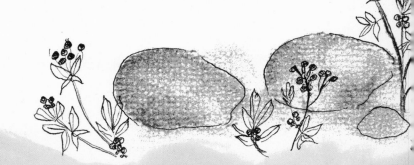

The Terrace

After a short rest, you continue to walk
down the mountain until you reach a place
where the slope is almost level, like a terrace.
On the terrace is a thick carpet of soil
covered with ferns.
The ferns are growing in clay soil.

Some clay has been washed down from the mountaintop,
some has washed from soil and weathered rock
on the mountain slope,
but most of the clay has come from a rock cliff
that once—long, long ago—made a high wall
at the back of the terrace.

During many rainy seasons, more than you can count,
water poured over the cliff
from the mountaintop above.
The cliff rock became worn and weathered.
As the cliff weathered and crumbled,
much of the sand was washed and blown away.

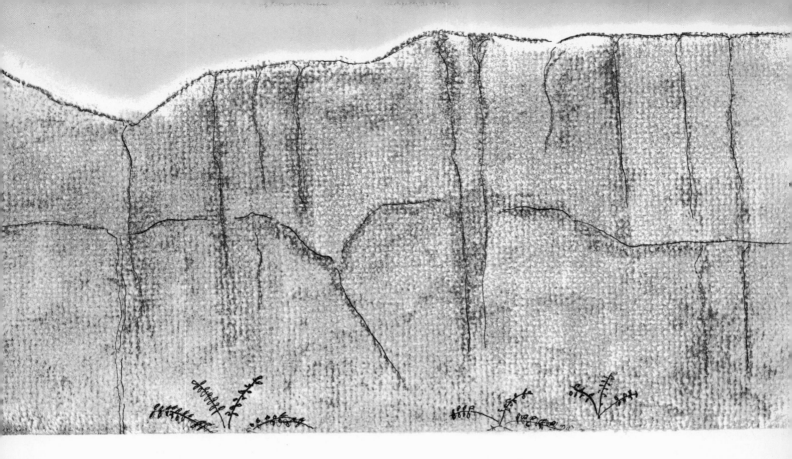

The rotting feldspar was left, changing to clay.
Now the cliff is only a high bank.
The bank looks like gray rock,
but it is powdery
and it crumbles under your feet
when you try to climb it.

Now you leave the terrace
and start down the mountain slope again.
You are no longer traveling through ferns;
your feet are not scuffing through dusty clay.
Now you are walking on spongy, damp soil.

Willows and hemlocks are growing around you.
Here clay and sandy soil
are holding some of the rain water
that came from the top of the mountain,
but there is also a tiny stream
winding its way between root hummocks.
Where is this stream coming from?
It is bubbling out of the ground
near the bottom of the clay bank.
Put your hand in the water.
How cold it is! This is a spring.

When rain water falls or flows
onto a carpet of growing plants,
or seeps into clay soil,
the water is held as if in a sponge.
Spongy soil stores the rain water,
sometimes for weeks, sometimes for years.
When rain water soaks into spongy soil
until it can hold no more,
the water seeps out of the ground.

Sometimes, water overflows through a crack in a rock,
or from a place where sand and gravel have collected.
When water overflows from a place
where it has been stored, the water makes a spring.
Water is flowing from this spring,
making several tiny paths.
The paths join to make a brook.

You see pebbles, sand, and small pieces of rock in the brook.
The pieces of rock are being worn smooth
by moving sand and water.
Some pieces of rock will become pebbles which—
as they grind and crash against each other—
will become smoother and smaller
until they are grains of sand.
You can find many pieces of rock in the brook
being changed to sand.
Take a stick and stir up some of the pebbles,
mud, and sand that lie at the bottom of the brook.
The pebbles will fall back to the bottom,
but watch the sand and mud.
The moving water carries some soil farther down the brook.
You can see places where water has washed soil away
from the roots of trees growing on the brook bank.

Some soil will be deposited farther down the brook,
some will be carried to the river in the valley,
and the river will carry some of that soil
all the way down to the ocean.
Every day, wind and water
are carrying soil to the ocean.
It takes many, many years for soil to travel
from the mountain to the ocean,
because there are many, many stopping-off places.
Here the brook bank slopes down
to a muddy flat place beside shallow water.
This is a watering place for animals.
There are tiny clawmarks
where a raccoon came to wash its food,
and here are the heart-shaped hoofprints of a deer.
Let's follow the hoofmarks.

The deerprints lead up over the brook bank,
back onto the mountain slope.

Now you are walking on firm, dry soil
because this soil contains more sand and less clay.
Sand is like a sieve, and water drains off easily
between its hard, small grains.
Grass is growing here in the sandy soil,
and there is a narrow path where leaves
have been nibbled from overhanging branches.
Here and there, you can see more hoofmarks.

The deer made a trail as it hunted for food
and shelter on the mountain.
The deer trail leads through wild blackberry bushes
and stalks of milkweed,
then between slender young maple trees
where there are tender twigs for the deer to eat.
Beyond the saplings there are many dark, straight trunks—
so many that they look like an army of trees.

The Forest

How different it is from the top of the mountain.
You walk on a thick, soft carpet of soil.
The air is cool.
The ground does not get much sunlight,
because it is shaded by the leaves of trees.
Year after year, leaves have fallen from the trees.

Dig under the leaves, into the soil,
and see what you can find.
There are pieces of roots and twigs.
You may find bits of fur and bones of animals
that died in the woods;
feathers and droppings of birds
that fly through the forest;
eggshells, snakeskins, snail shells, butterfly wings,
old cocoons, pieces of bark, and stumps of trees.

These things remain on the ground
all autumn and all winter—
through warm days, cold days, dry days, wet days,
through season after season.
Like the rock on the mountain, they slowly weather,
crumble, and change to soil—
another kind of soil, called humus.
Humus is made of all things, or parts of things,
that you can think of that have ever lived.

Here, on a dead stump,
is a kind of plant called fungus.
It is curved and looks like a dark red shelf.
This is a bracket fungus.
Fungi grow on old stumps, logs, and on dead trees.
They feed on the dead wood, breaking it down,
making it soft and crumbly.
Then the rotted wood, too, is added to the soil.
Mushrooms and toadstools are fungi also.
They grow on logs, under leaves,
and around the roots of trees.
They make things crumble too.

One kind of fungus is so tiny that we can't see it.
These invisible fungi are bacteria.
Bacteria that live in the soil are called
garbage removers because they remove all the refuse—
dead insects, old fur, bark, bones, dead animals, everything!
There are so many bacteria that more than a billion
live in a lump of forest soil the size of a coat button.
Bacteria remove garbage wherever they find it, by changing it.
They manufacture chemicals that slowly break down
and change all the garbage into humus.
This change is called decay.
All the things that you find on the forest floor
are slowly breaking down and decaying—making humus.
The humus is filled with plant food.
When it is mixed with minerals from rock, it becomes soil,
full of nourishment for all growing things.

Insects mix the soil too.
They carry bits of leaves and soil
from one place to another.
Worms, beetles, flies, and crickets tunnel down
through the damp soil.
Spiders and daddy longlegs crawl through the tunnels.

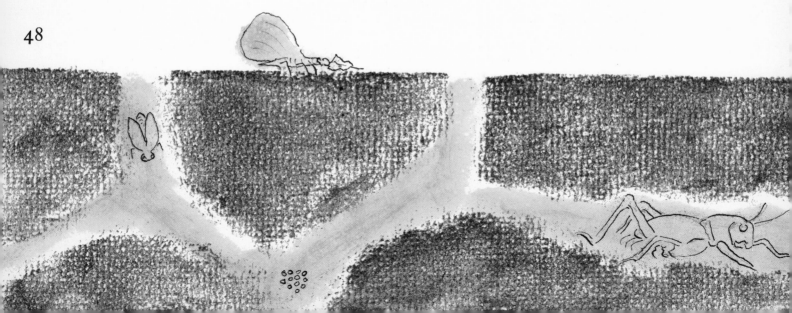

They hunt for food, find shelter,
and lay eggs within the tunnels.
These tunnels and trails make busy highways
that crisscross all through the soil.
The insects eat and eat and eat.
They grind, mix, and mash bones
and other things in the soil.
While all this is going on,
bacteria help the things to rot and decay.

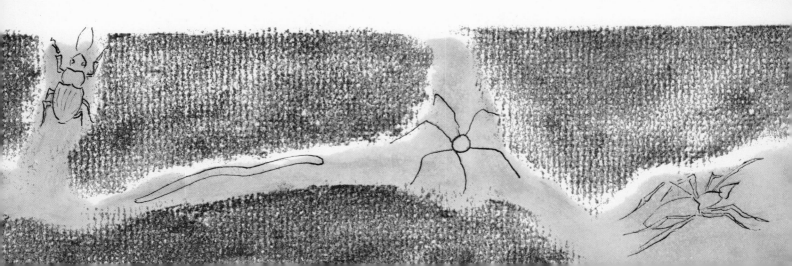

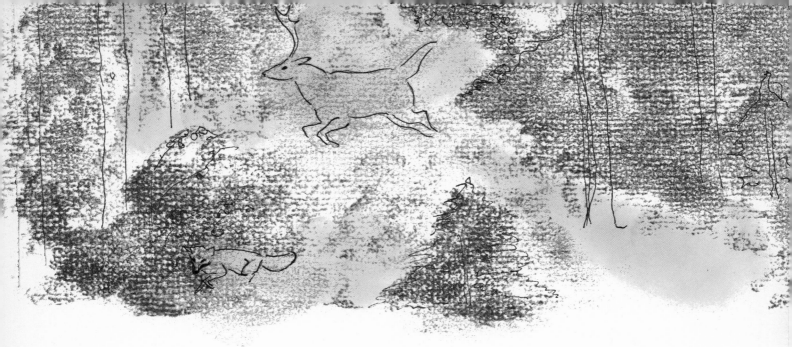

As you walk through the forest,
you can find narrow trails winding in and out
through the underbrush.
Many animals travel through the forest.
They also help to crumble things that are in the soil.
In some places, deer and bear trample twigs and leaves.
The fox, rabbit, and porcupine make trails
under and through the leaves.

Snakes, toads and lizards go over and under the leaves.
They burrow into the soil,
leaving more and more droppings.
Everywhere, animals are mixing and adding to the soil,
while billions of insects and bacteria help
to decay the waste that the animals leave.
Even as you walk through the forest,
you are, in a small way, helping the process of decay.

The Meadow

Beyond the edge of the forest,
near the foot of the mountain, you come to a meadow.
Long before you were born,
this meadow was a forest
and a hunting place for birds and animals.
There was a deep layer of humus,
rich with food for plants.

Early settlers, searching for a place to live,
camped by the brook and discovered the rich soil.
The settlers felled the trees to make their cabins.
Roots that held the soil were burned.
Rocks were piled up into stone walls.
The settlers planted crops on the cleared land.
Year after year, they harvested corn and wheat
from the soil.

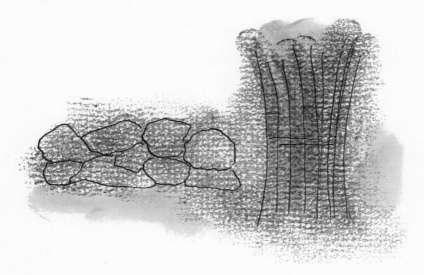

Minerals and food materials from the rich soil
were used by the plants year after year.
It became harder and harder
for the settlers to grow good crops,
because the plant food in the soil was being used up.
Finally, the settlers had to move
to other forest land.

It will take a long time
for a beech or a maple tree to grow
in this meadow again.
Trees grow slowly.
It will be many years before there is underbrush
in which animals can hunt and find shelter.
Only a few bushes are growing in this sandy meadow,
but their roots will now hold the rain and soil.
Each fall, leaves and seeds will fall to the ground.
Each spring, a few new plants will grow.
Perhaps birds will nest here again
and bring seeds for more plants.
Perhaps animals will return for food and shelter.
Slowly the soil will change
and, after many, many years, a new forest will grow.

A narrow, sunny path leads through the meadow
to a brook where animals go to drink.
This is the brook that you left partway up the mountain,
but it has changed—it is wide.
More springs and streams joined the brook
as it flowed down the mountain.
The water flows deep and quietly here.

You can look through the clear water
and see a layer of sand at the bottom of the brook.
Perhaps this is a stopping-off place
for some of the sand
that came way from the top of the mountain.
It is a stopping-off place for you too.

A Million Years from Now

What a discovering trip you have had!
You have found grains of sand
made from the quartz in weathered rock.
You have found clay
made from rotted, crumbled feldspar and mica,
and you have found rich, soft humus
made from decaying things in the forest.

You can find sand, clay, and humus in other places too.
Whenever you go for a walk in a forest,
take some soil in your hands and examine it.
Is it soft and crumbly?
How many things can you find in it
that are changing into food for plants?
Whenever you walk along a beach beside the ocean
or a lake or a river, take some sand in your hand.
Let it sift between your fingers.
Can you see the tiny, hard grains of quartz?
Perhaps you can find rock
that some of the sand came from.
Look for clay banks
along brooks, rivers, and roadways.
If the clay is wet, it will be sticky.
You can mold maps, castles, and animals out of wet clay.

When you walk on a grassy place,
dig under the grass a little.
Perhaps there, in the soil,
you will find small pieces of rock so rotten
that they crumble in your fingers.
You may find an old weathered piece of board.
If you turn it over, you'll probably see
a beetle running away from the light,
a worm or grub curling under cover,
or a colony of ants scurrying to protect their eggs.

You may see all these things within a tiny patch of soil.
Think of bigger places—forests, garbage heaps, and gardens.
In all these bigger places,
billions and billions of insects and bacteria
are changing and mixing the waste materials.
Wherever you walk, you can find things
slowly changing into sand, clay, or humus.
Every day, every minute, rock is breaking down.
Every minute, every day, weather, plants, and animals
are changing things into soil
and bacteria are helping to decay the waste.
These changes are so slow and so small
that we cannot see them happening.
But we have discovered how changes happen
by exploring one mountain.

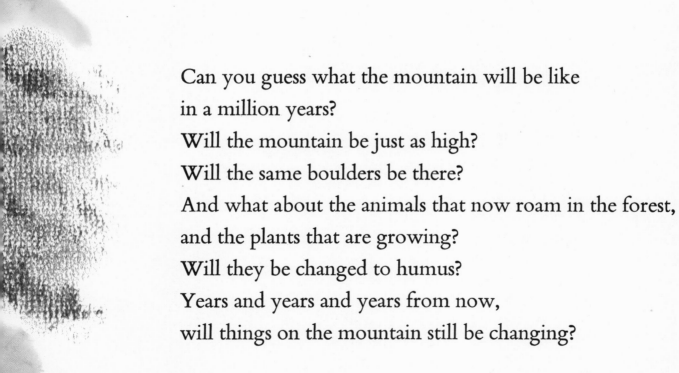

Can you guess what the mountain will be like
in a million years?
Will the mountain be just as high?
Will the same boulders be there?
And what about the animals that now roam in the forest,
and the plants that are growing?
Will they be changed to humus?
Years and years and years from now,
will things on the mountain still be changing?

Margaret Farrington Bartlett

Although Margaret Farrington Bartlett, as coordinator of the science department at the Dalton School in New York City, works with children and teachers of all ages, her favorite area is the very young age level where native curiosity is unhampered and children are freely responsive to exploring experiences.

Miss Bartlett has written many magazine articles about science for teachers and several science books for beginning readers. In addition to writing and teaching, she has achieved recognition as a painter and has had a number of one-man shows throughout the East.

Miss Bartlett spends her winters in New York City teaching and writing and her summers writing and painting on a Vermont mountain top.

Rhys Caparn

It is a privilege, by means of the drawings in this book, to introduce children to the work of Rhys Caparn. Miss Caparn is a distinguished sculptor whose work is widely represented in public and private collections throughout the United States and Europe.

Miss Caparn is President of the Federation of Modern Painters and Sculptors, a Fellow of the International Institute of Arts and Letters, Second Prize winner in the comprehensive exhibition of American Sculpture held at the Metropolitan Museum of Art in 1951, and recipient in 1960 and 1961 of the Medal of Honor for Sculpture from the National Association of Women Artists.